Best *of* *the* **West** *Biographies*

Jesse James
Wild West Train Robber

Elaine Landau

E **Enslow Publishers, Inc.**

40 Industrial Road   PO Box 38
Box 398   Aldershot
Berkeley Heights, NJ 07922   Hants GU12 6BP
USA   UK

http://www.enslow.com

Library of Congress Cataloging-in-Publication Data

Landau, Elaine.
    Jesse James : Wild West train robber / Elaine Landau.
        p. cm. — (Best of the West biographies)
        Summary: A biography of the outlaw who, with his brother Frank, led a gang of bank and train robbers from the late 1860's through the 1870's.
        Includes bibliographical references and index.
        ISBN 0-7660-2208-0 (hardcover)
        1. James, Jesse, 1847–1882—Juvenile literature.
    2. Outlaws—West (U.S.)—Biography—Juvenile literature.
    3. Frontier and pioneer life—West (U.S.)—Juvenile literature.
    4. West (U.S.)—History—1860-1890—Juvenile literature. 5. West (U.S.)—Biography—Juvenile literature. [1. James, Jesse, 1847–1882. 2. Robbers and outlaws. 3. Frontier and pioneer life—West (U.S.) 4. West (U.S.)—History—1860–1890.] I. Title. II. Series.
        F594.J27L36 2004
        978'.02'092—dc21
                                        2003010335

Printed in the United States of America

10 9 8 7 6 5 4 3 2 1

To Our Readers: We have done our best to make sure that all Internet addresses in this book were active and appropriate when we went to press. However, the author and publisher have no control over and assume no liability for the material available on those Internet sites or on other Web sites they may link to. Any comments or suggestions can be sent by e-mail to comments@enslow.com or to the address on the back cover.

Photo Credits: AP/Wide World Photos, p. 8, 19, 31, 34, 38, 39, 40; © Corel Corporation, pp. 1, 2–3, 5, 10, 18, 23 (background), 24, 30, 36; Hemera Technologies, Inc., p. 6; Enslow Publishers, Inc., pp. 4, 14; Photos.com, p. 20; National Archives and Records Administration, pp. 15, 33, 37; Reproduced from the Collections of the Library of Congress, pp. 7, 12, 16, 21, 23, 25, 28, 32; Reproduced from the *Dictionary of American Portraits*, published by Dover Publications, Inc., p. 27; State Historical Society of Missouri , p. 29; Western History Collection, University of Oklahoma, p. 11.

Cover Photos: © Corel Corporation (Background); AP/Wide World Photos (Portrait).

Contents

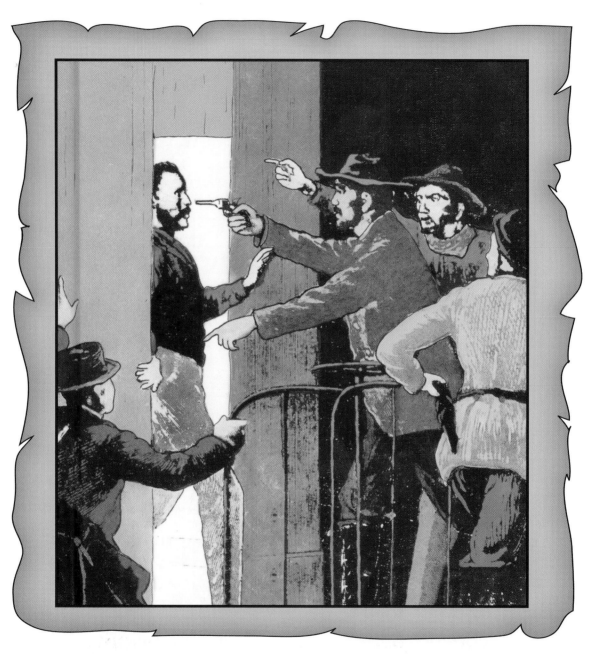

Jesse James and his gang often made daring train robberies.

The Unforgettable Ride

It was a hot July day in 1873. Things were quiet in the Iowa countryside. The only sound was the rumble of passing trains. One was on its way now. It had just passed the town of Adair. The Chicago, Rock Island, and Pacific Railroad was running on time.

But something was terribly wrong that afternoon. The engineer spotted the danger ahead. Part of the track was torn away. The engineer had to think fast. He tried to back up the train. But it was too late.

Seconds later, the engine spun off the track. The cars behind it came to a screeching halt. Some passengers were thrown from their seats.

The engine toppled over, as well. It crushed the engineer's body.

A group of young men rushed onto the train. They seemed to come out of nowhere. The men were not passengers. They were not there to help, either. These men wore masks. They were train robbers.

The robbers had caused the train wreck. Earlier that day, they had loosened some rails on the track. They tied the end of the rails to long ropes. When they saw the train coming, they pulled on the ropes. The track broke apart.

The men wasted no time. Some walked directly to the baggage car. They quickly went through the boxes and suitcases. The robbers tossed clothing, books, and tools in all directions. Anything of value was snatched.

It was easy for Jesse's men to go through the bags. There were no such things as baggage locks.

Trains were used to transport almost anything, from people and goods, to money and mail.

The other outlaws were busy, as well. They were robbing the passengers at gunpoint. The frightened train riders did as they were told. They quickly handed over their money, watches, and rings.

Jesse was widely known for committing all kinds of robberies.

This train was supposed to be carrying a large gold shipment. However, the gold was not there. The shipment had been put on a later train. Still, the men did not leave empty-handed. They rode off with several thousand dollars in cash and jewelry.

The people of J̶... ̶ked. So was the ... been bank robb... held up, as well. ... oving train to be ro...

T... ̶pset. It want... en captured. Findi... would not be ea... do just that for ye...

The gang leader was already a well-known outlaw. Some people admired him. They often helped him hide. Others saw him as a thief and killer. But no matter what they thought of him, everyone knew his name. He was Jesse James.

I could yous that ↓

Jesse Woodson James was not born an outlaw. His father, Robert Salle James, was a Baptist minister. Robert preached on Sundays. During the week, he worked on his farm in Kearney, Missouri. Jesse's mother, Zerelda, helped on the farm. The couple's slaves worked there, too. The James family had come to Missouri from Kentucky. They had brought their slaves with them.

Jesse James was born on the family farm on September 5, 1847. He had an older brother named Frank. Later, his younger sister, Susan, was born. Jesse's family was happy. But their happiness did not last.

In 1848, gold was discovered in California.

Thousands flocked there. Everyone hoped to strike it rich. Unfortunately, Robert Salle James was among them. He set out hoping for the best. Instead, the worst happened. Jesse's father never became rich. Three weeks after leaving, he became very ill. He died shortly thereafter.

Jesse's mother remarried in 1852. Her new husband was a wealthy farmer named Ben Simms. That marriage did not last. Frank and Jesse did not like Simms. Simms did not care for them, either. The couple decided to separate. But just before they did, Simms died.

Three years later, Jesse's mother married once again.

Jesse James's mother lived until she was eighty-six years old.

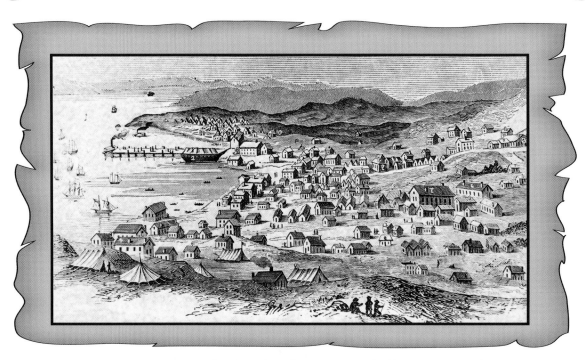

Large numbers of people flocked to San Francisco during the California Gold Rush. It soon became a bustling city.

Her third husband was Dr. Rueben Samuel. He was a kind man and a good doctor. Samuel got along well with the children, too. Rueben and Zerelda had four children together. Jesse was also close to his half brothers and sisters.

Now Jesse's home life was calm. But the surrounding area was not. Some people in western Missouri were in favor of slavery.

Jesse's family was among them. Others in the region were firmly against it.

Over time, more settlers moved to nearby Kansas. The slavery argument spread, as well. So did the anger. At times, fighting broke out between the people for and against slavery. As a teenager, Jesse James was surrounded by fighting and bloodshed.

In 1861, things worsened. The Civil War started. Southerners wanted to continue their way of life. That meant keeping slavery. The Southern states tried to leave the Union. The North fought to keep the nation together and to do away with slavery.

Missouri sided with the North. But many people in Jesse's area believed in the South. Some of these men refused to join the Union, or Northern army. They wanted to help the South any way they could. Often, they formed bands of raiders. These men became known as bushwhackers. They did not fight openly as soldiers. Instead, they tried to surprise the enemy troops.

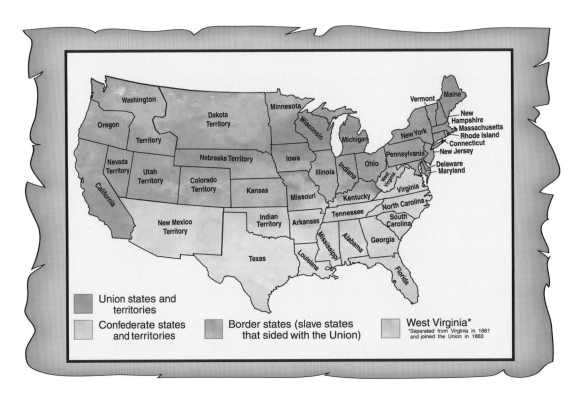

The following states and territories are shown on the map:

Union states and territories

Confederate states and territories

Border states (slave states that sided with the Union)

West Virginia*
*Separated from Virginia in 1861 and joined the Union in 1863

The Civil War sharply divided the nation.

The bushwhackers often struck at night. They destroyed bridges and telegraph wires. The men burned Union storage bins and attacked small patrols of Northern soldiers. They also robbed banks and businesses in Union towns.

In 1862, Jesse's older brother, Frank, became a bushwhacker. Frank joined a group

known as Quantrill's Raiders. Jesse wanted to join, too. But he was too young. He had to wait two years. When Jesse turned sixteen in 1864, he was accepted.

Jesse's unit commander was a man called "Bloody Bill" Anderson. Jesse was one of Bloody Bill's youngest raiders. Some thought of Jesse as a boy. He was slim and had a youthful face. But Jesse fought like a man. He was never seen without his guns. His blue eyes seemed filled with hate, as well.

By early 1865, the war was nearly over. One thing was clear. The South was

It was Jesse's older brother, Frank, who acted as a role model to Jesse. He joined his first outlaw group two years before Jesse was old enough to follow.

losing. Jesse and some other raiders tried to surrender. The men slowly approached a Union patrol on horseback. Jesse was at the front of the line. He carried a white flag. That showed that they were giving up. But one Union solider

Banks like this one became one of Jesse's favorite targets for robberies.

in the group did not care. He shot Jesse in the chest.

Jesse nearly died. His cousin, Zee Mimms, nursed him back to health. Zee's real name was Zerelda. She was named after Jesse's mother. Months passed before Jesse was well. During this time, Zee and Jesse became very close.

After the war, Jesse had to make some decisions. How was he going to spend his life? Jesse hated farming. He wanted no part of it. He had not been trained for much else.

As a bushwhacker, Jesse had robbed Union banks and businesses. He knew how to shoot. He could make a quick getaway, too. He decided to continue on this path. He would rather steal than work. It was as simple as that. Jesse James became an outlaw.

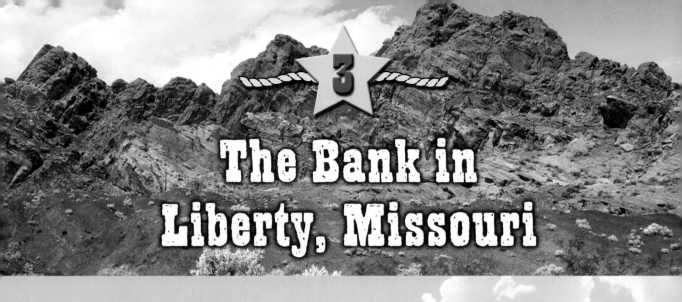

The Bank in Liberty, Missouri

Bank robberies were common during the Civil War. Many people knew of them. But few had ever heard of a bank robbery during peace time. And nobody had heard of a bank robbery in broad daylight! Everyone thought banks were safe. Jesse James would prove them wrong.

James was a planner. He was also someone who did not work alone. James put together an outlaw gang. All the men in the gang had been bushwhackers. All still hated the North.

James's older brother Frank was part of the group. So was their friend Cole Younger. Younger brought in his brothers Bob, John, and James. Several other young men joined, too.

James usually picked their targets. The first

was the Clay County Savings Bank. It was in Liberty, Missouri. That was just miles from where James was born. James picked that bank for a reason. It was owned by Northerners.

The robbery took place on February 13, 1866. The James gang met early that morning.

This building was the site of the Clay County Savings Bank robbery, one of Jesse's most profitable hold-ups.

During the Civil War, Union soldiers wore dark blue uniforms and the Confederate soldiers wore gray.

They put on Union soldier uniforms and masks. Then, they loaded their guns and rode into town.

Only two of the men went into the bank. The others stayed outside. They were lookouts.

The bank cashiers were a father and son named Greenup and William Cage. They were working when the robbers walked in. The robbers held them up at gunpoint.

The outlaws told the Cages to keep quiet. They made them hand over the money in the teller's cage. They also wanted whatever was in the vault. However, they did not leave the vault empty. Before going, the outlaws locked the Cages in it. They left with over $60,000 in coins, cash, and bonds.

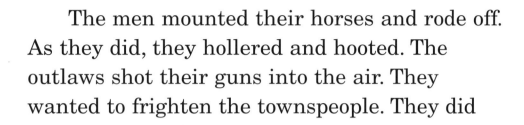

The men mounted their horses and rode off. As they did, they hollered and hooted. The outlaws shot their guns into the air. They wanted to frighten the townspeople. They did not want to be followed.

Jesse and his gang wanted to make a quick escape after robbing the Clay County Savings Bank. Much like the cowboys in the above drawing, the James gang galloped out of town.

People on the street quickly ran for cover. But a college student named George Wyne was not fast enough. He was killed by a stray bullet.

The town's sheriff formed a posse. A posse is a group of men that help lawmen go after outlaws. The posse tried to bring in the robbers. They did not succeed. Not a single gang member was caught.

That day helped make the James gang famous. They had pulled off the first daytime bank robbery since the war. People talked about it for months. The Union uniforms and masks had not fooled everyone. A few people recognized some of the gang members. They were amazed at their daring. That was the gang's first job. It would not be their last.

Present or Absent?

Did Jesse James really rob the bank in Liberty, Missouri? His gang is known for it. However, the outlaws were masked. Outlaws of the day often wore masks when they robbed stagecoaches or banks. Can anyone be sure who was at the bank in Liberty? History experts disagree about where James was that day. Some say he was one of the lookouts outside the bank. Others believe that James was not there at all. They think he was still too weak from his chest wound. Perhaps he just helped plan the robbery.

Hero or Villain?

In time, Jesse James became a well-known outlaw. His gang held up banks, trains, and stagecoaches. When the situation became too dangerous in Missouri, he went elsewhere. The James gang also robbed in Kentucky, Iowa, Arkansas, Texas, Kansas, Minnesota, Colorado, Illinois, and Alabama.

Jesse James was an outlaw. But not everyone thought he was bad. This was especially true of farmers. Many farmers disliked banks and railroads. During hard times, some farmers missed payments on their land. When this happened, the banks often took away their farms. The railroads also made it hard for farmers. They charged

extrem[...] costly for
farmer[...]

Th[...] turn
Jesse [...]s, many of
these [...]. Now they
called [...] Robin Hood."
They [...]eeds. They
said t[...] the rich and
gave t[...]

> *like Robin Hood*
>
> *Robbed from the rich on gave to the poor*

THE GREAT TRAIN ROBBERY

SENSATIONAL AND STARTLING "HOLD UP" OF THE "GOLD EXPRESS", BY FAMOUS WESTERN OUTLAWS

Robbing trains was only one of the many crimes Jesse and his men committed.

That made for interesting reading. People liked having a local hero. But none of it was true. Jesse James liked money. He usually kept what he had stolen. Innocent people were also killed during his robberies. James did not care. He always said that they should not have tried to stop him.

Of course, not everyone admired James. The railroads and banks wanted him caught. They hired the Pinkerton National Detective Agency to bring him in. This was a private agency. Its men were well known. They had captured many dangerous outlaws.

In early 1874, Pinkerton agent John Whicher went to Missouri. He wanted to get a job on the farm that belonged to Jesse James's stepfather. He hoped to find James that way. Whicher did not get very far. He was later found shot to death.

The Pinkertons did not give up. Two agents hid out near Rueben Samuel's farm. They were waiting for Jesse and Frank James. The brothers sometimes visited their mother there.

Allan Pinkerton worked as a spy for the Union during the Civil War. Here, he stands with Abraham Lincoln.

They watched the farm for two days. Then they heard that the James brothers were on their way home. They were to arrive after sundown on January 26, 1875. That evening, Pinkerton agents surrounded the farmhouse. They yelled for the brothers to come out. No one left the house. Only a light in the window went out.

The Pinkertons did not wait any longer. They tossed a bomb through the window. The loud explosion shook the ground. The results were terrible. A young half-brother was killed.

Jesse's mother was also hurt. Her arm later had to be cut off.

The public was angry. Newspapers called the Pinkertons monsters. People were outraged because James's half-brother was only a child. Everyone felt sorry for the James family.

The Pinkerton National Detective Agency could not stop Jesse James. He and his gang went on robbing. James became even better known. Some people began to call Missouri the "Bandit State." This embarrassed Missouri Governor Thomas T. Crittenden. He offered a $5,000 reward for James's capture. That was a lot of money in those days. It made life even more dangerous for Jesse James.

As the governor of Missouri, Thomas Crittenden wanted Jesse and his men put in jail.

Even with prices on their heads, no one turned in Jesse or any of his men to the law.

Despite the danger, James still had a family of his own. He had married his cousin Zee Mimms on April 23, 1874. The couple later had two children. There was a boy named Jesse, Jr., and a girl named Mary. Zee knew the truth about her husband. She had married a bandit. Zee did not like what James did. She often feared for his safety. Yet she remained loyal to him to the end.

PROCLAMATION
$5,000⁰⁰
REWARD
FOR EACH of SEVEN ROBBERS of THE TRAIN at WINSTON, MO., JULY 15, 1881, and THE MURDER of CONDUCTER WESTFALL
$ 5,000.00
ADDITIONAL for ARREST or CAPTURE
DEAD OR ALIVE
OF JESSE OR FRANK JAMES
THIS NOTICE TAKES the PLACE of ALL PREVIOUS REWARD NOTICES.
CONTACT SHERIFF, DAVIESS COUNTY, MISSOURI IMMEDIATELY
T. T. CRITTENDEN, GOVERNOR
STATE OF MISSOURI
JULY 26, 1881

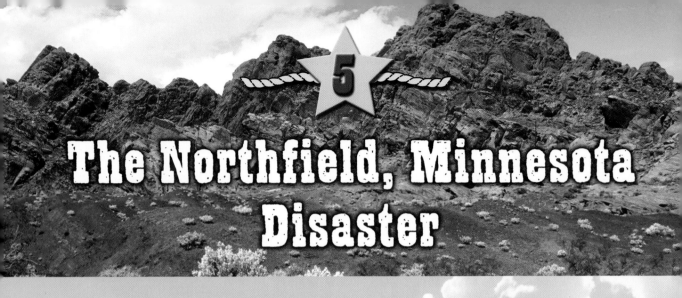

The Northfield, Minnesota Disaster

Outlaws had to be prepared for anything. It was the only way they could survive. Sometimes, being prepared meant being well-armed. Each member of the James gang carried a short-barreled rifle. Two Colt pistols also hung from their gun belts. Jesse James did even more. He wore shoulder holsters. There were two extra pistols in these.

But being well-armed was not always enough. Jesse James was not prepared for what happened on September 8, 1876. That was the day the James gang came to Northfield, Minnesota. They were there to rob the bank.

Minnesota was not like Missouri. Bandit gangs were uncommon there. Northfield looked

like other towns the James gang had been to. But it was different. These townspeople were hard-working pioneers. They valued honesty. They also greatly respected the law. Outlaws who rode into Northfield were in for trouble. The locals were prepared to fight them.

The gang should have never gone to Northfield. The trouble started right away. First, the bank cashier refused to open the safe. The townspeople quickly realized what was happening. They grabbed their rifles and began to shoot the outlaws waiting outside the bank.

Jesse was in the bank. Some other gang members were with him. They heard the gunfire outside.

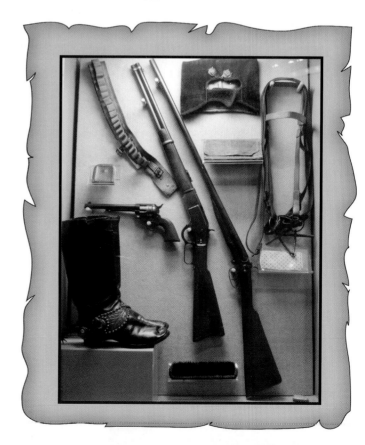

These are Jesse's rifles and the boots he wore when he was killed.

Going west often meant living in small log cabins like this one away from any help or people.

The men knew they had to get away. They grabbed a few dollars from the cash drawer. Then, they headed for the door. But before leaving, the outlaws did one more thing. They shot the bank cashier in the head.

The street outside looked like a battlefield. Bullets flew in all directions. One of Jesse's men was hit in the chest. He fell off his horse and died. Another was shot in the face. He died minutes later. Cole Younger took a bullet in the shoulder. His brothers, Bob and Jim, were wounded as well.

Only Jesse and Frank were unharmed. They and the wounded members of the gang rode off. As they left, the townspeople were still shooting at them. Even those without guns tried to help. They threw rocks at the fleeing robbers.

Afterwards, the James gang split up. This gave them a better chance of

The Younger brothers, pictured here with their sister, Henrietta. From the left they are: Bob, Jim, and Cole. All were original members of the James gang.

This statue in Stanton, Missouri, marks one of
Jesse's favorite hiding places. He liked it so much
because he could safely hide all his men and their
horses there.

escaping. Jesse and Frank James got away. Lawmen tracked down the Younger brothers. Once their wounds healed, they stood trial. The men were sentenced to life in prison.

The Northfield raid made Jesse James more famous than ever. Hundreds of lawmen now looked for him. Meanwhile, the James brothers had headed south. They traveled mostly at night. During the day, they hid in deserted barns and buildings. They ate what they could find in the wild.

Several weeks later, they arrived in Missouri. But it was too dangerous for them to stay very long. People had begun to think less of Jesse James. Too many people had died during his robberies. They were not always Northerners, either. It was getting harder to defend Jesse James's actions.

The Final Years

After the Northfield robbery, Jesse James lived quietly. He and his family sometimes stayed on a farm he bought in Tennessee. But James also moved his family to different places. This was important for his safety. Lawmen were still looking for him. He did not want to be caught.

About three years later, James's money ran low. So in 1879 he put together a new gang. He had to do this. Most of the old members were dead or in jail. As before, they robbed banks and trains. This further upset Governor Crittenden. He raised the award for James's capture. It was now set at $10,000.

James stayed on the move. In 1881, he and his family were living in St. Joseph, Missouri.

He used the name Thomas Howard there. None of his neighbors knew who he really was.

Robert and Charles Ford were members of James's new gang. The Ford brothers were not loyal. They wanted the reward money. They were willing to betray James to get it. The Fords knew that they could never bring Jesse James in alive. So, they decided to kill him.

On April 3, 1882, the Fords visited James. James thought they had come to discuss a robbery. But the Fords were really there to murder him.

The brothers waited until James took off his guns.

Robert Ford (pictured) and his brother, Charles, told people they were Jesse's cousins, but they really were not related to him at all.

When he turned to straighten a picture, Robert Ford made his move. He shot Jesse James in the back of the head at close range. The country's most famous outlaw was finally dead.

Or was he? Some people say that story is not true. They claim that the thirty-four-year-old outlaw faked his own death. That way, James could live freely. Another man was supposedly put in Jesse James's grave.

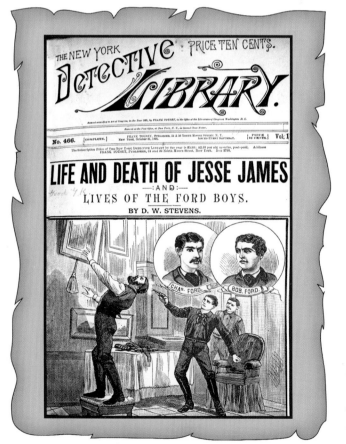

Since then, several men have claimed to be Jesse James. Each said he was the real outlaw. But many people thought the true Jesse James was a man in Granbury, Texas. His name was J. Frank Dalton. The J was said to stand for Jesse.

The Ford brothers killed Jesse because they wanted the reward money.

Jesse is buried next to his wife, Zerelda, in his birthplace—Kearny, Missouri. In life, Zerelda was usually called Zee. James's mother sold pebbles from his original gravesite as souvenirs to tourists.

Dalton was a name from Jesse's mother's side of the family. Frank was Jesse James's brother's name.

Dalton died in 1951 at the age of 103. Could he have really been Jesse James? Dalton looked a lot like James. He also knew many details

Top: Men dig up Jesse James's casket in 1995. Bottom: James's casket is guarded by two men pretending to be confederate soldiers.

about James's life. Some say that Dalton knew things only Jesse James could have known.

The debate went on for over forty years. Then in 1995, things were finally settled. Jesse James's body was dug up. It was taken from its grave in Kearney, Missouri. Scientists carefully studied James's remains. There was no longer any doubt. The real Jesse James had been killed in 1882.

However, Jesse James's legend lives on. There are yearly Jesse James festivals. Thousands of people also visit the farm where James was born. There have been many books and movies about him, as well. In these, he is often shown as a hero.

Others see Jesse James in a truer light. They want people to remember that James lived outside the law. Innocent people died during his robberies.

People may argue about Jesse's character. Yet one thing is certain. Jesse James has a place in western history. His story is still told today. It probably will be for some time to come.

Timeline

1847—Jesse Woodson James is born on September 5.

1848—Gold is struck in California. Jesse James's father heads west, but dies soon after.

1852—Jesse James's mother, Zerelda, marries her second husband.

1855—Zerelda James marries her third husband, Dr. Rueben Samuel.

1861—The Civil War begins.

1862—Jesse James's older brother, Frank, joins Quantrill's raiders.

1864—Jesse James joins Quantrill's raiders. He serves in "Bloody Bill" Anderson's unit.

1865—The Civil War ends.

1866—The James Gang robs the Clay County Savings Bank in Liberty, Missouri, on February 13.

1873—The James Gang pulls off its first train robbery near Adair, Iowa, on July 21.

1874—Jesse James marries his cousin, Zee Mimms, on April 23.

1875—Agents from the Pinkerton National Detective Agency bomb the Samuel farm on January 26. Jesse James's half-brother is killed. His mother is hurt, as well.

1876—The James Gang robs the bank in Northfield, Minnesota, on September 8. The robbery fails and some gang members are killed.

1879—Jesse James puts together a new gang. Its members include brothers Robert and Charles Ford.

1881—Jesse James moves his family to St. Joseph, Missouri.

1882—Robert Ford kills Jesse James on April 3.

Words to Know

baggage—Suitcases, bags, and trunks used by travelers.

bandit—A robber who uses a weapon.

bushwhackers—Small bands of Southern raiders in the Civil War.

capture—To take someone or something by force.

Civil War—The war between the North and South that took place in the United States between 1861 and 1865.

debate—To argue or discuss.

engineer—A person who drives a train.

freight—Goods carried on a train.

holster—A holder for a gun.

loyal—Faithful.

outlaw—A criminal who is running from punishment.

patrols—Small units of soldiers.

pioneer—A settler in a new region.

pistol—A small gun or firearm.

posse—A group of people who help a lawman catch an outlaw.

raid—A sudden, unexpected attack.

sheriff—A lawman.

Union soldiers—Northern troops who fought in the Civil War.

victim—A person who has been hurt or killed.

Reading About Jesse James

Blackwood, Gary L. *Outlaws*. Tarrytown, New York: Marshall Cavendish, 2001.

De Angelis, Gina. *The Wild West*. Broomall, Penn.: Chelsea House, 1999.

Marvis, B. and Richard Worth. *Great Robberies*. Broomall, Penn.: Chelsea House, 2000.

Murdoch, David Hamilton. *Eyewitness: Cowboy*. New York: DK Publishing, 2000.

Saffer. Barbara. *Jesse James*. Broomall, Penn.: Chelsea House, 2002.

Savage, Douglass J. *Rangers, Jayhawkers, and Bushwhackers in the Civil War*. Broomall, Penn.: Chelsea House, 2000.

Stanchak, John E. *Civil War*. New York: DK Publishing, 2000.